To Christine,
who believed so much in me,
I started believing, too

the BREAK-UP ACTIVITY BOOK
Crafting your way through *a Broken Heart*

by Lynn Chang

PROSPECT
·PARK·
BOOKS

The views expressed in this book are solely those of the author, and she means no harm by them. Even if you once broke her heart.

PROSPECT
·PARK·
BOOKS

Published by Prospect Park Books
969 S. Raymond Avenue
Pasadena, California 91105
www.prospectparkbooks.com

Library of Congress Control Number: 2012948390

The following is for reference only:
Chang, Lynn
The break-up activity book / by Lynn Chang — 1st ed.
p.cm.
ISBN: 978-1-938849-04-6
1. American wit and humor. I. Title.

First edition, first printing

Manufactured in China

ACKNOWLEDGMENTS

I would like to thank everyone who has worked to put this book together, particularly Colleen Dunn Bates, my editor and publisher, for her enthusiam and great sense of humor, and for getting me back into one of my first loves, which is writing silly books.

Special thanks to my fabulous photographer, Ronald Dunlap, and to Bethany Mendenhall, for their tireless support as friends and co-creative conspirators, and to Tony Mackay and Mohamed J. Semri for their indispensable help with ping-pong balls and jock straps, respectively.

Last but not least, my gratitude goes to my husband, Fox, for his enduring love and for not breaking my heart—not that he would dare to after reading this book.

Table of Contents

Table of Contents

Introduction

So you broke up and your heart is broken. Join the party baby, because you're not the only one. This year alone, 13 million people will shed salty tears for someone who is truly unworthy.

The heartbreak process is devastating for a while, but you'll survive. I created this book to help see you through the tough spots and inspire some therapeutic laughter. It is conveniently divided into three sections—Activities for the Despairing, Anger, Anger Anger, and Rejoining the Living—so wherever you are in the journey, you'll find something to give you focus and help you let go of your misery, rage, and anxiety. Plus it will keep your mind and hands busy, thereby reducing the time available for Facebook stalking and drunk dialing.

It doesn't matter if you're reduced to a sobbing, hysterical mess right now—you will get better. Really.

He didn't deserve you anyway,

Lynn

p.s. Don't cut your hair.

"A journey of a thousand miles must begin with a single step."
— Lao-Tsu

Getting Started

It turns out that the best way to get started on anything, even the road to recovery, is to just get started. So it's time to break out those nifty crafting supplies that likely have been languishing in forgotten boxes, gathering a fine sheen of dust. If you are a crafting novice, this is a great excuse to engage in some retail therapy and release your inner creative child. You'll be surprised to see how far crafting has come since your crayon-drawing days.

Most of the crafts in this book are easily made with things found around the house, but you should make sure to at least have the following on hand:

- Adhesives: glue gun + glue gun sticks, white glue, glue stick, needle/thread
- Cutting tools: scissors, exacto knife + blades, razor-sharp butcher knife (just kidding)
- Colorful construction paper
- Small pliers
- Deep well of anger, sadness, and (later) empowerment

MONTH 1

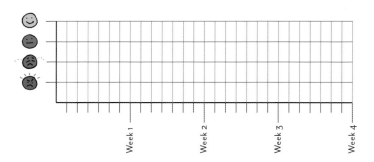

Week 1   Week 2   Week 3   Week 4

MONTH 2

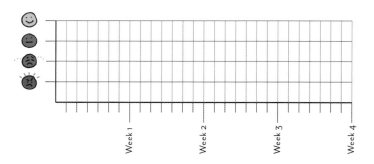

Week 1   Week 2   Week 3   Week 4

MONTH 3

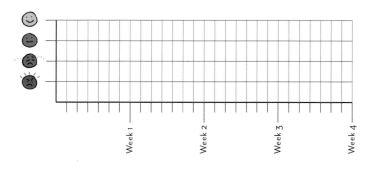

Week 1   Week 2   Week 3   Week 4

Mapping Your Progress

There's nothing quite like seeing on paper how emotionally schizophrenic you are after a break up, so we've created this handy chart to illustrate the journey.

The goal, however, is not to feel badly about how wildly your moods are swinging—instead, look at it as a badge of honor *(see Certificates of Completion on pages 102-103)* for having gone through it. Know that even though it doesn't feel like it's possible right now, one day, you will be so over it.

Analysis - Month 1

- -

- -

- -

Analysis - Month 2

- -

- -

- -

Analysis - Month 3

- -

- -

- -

Peanut Gallery

Sometimes you feel like a nut

When your broken heart craves advice but cannot bear the usual well-meaning but nevertheless annoying (even homicide-inducing) input from family and friends, we have the answer: Solicit nurturing support from your own personal Peanut Gallery.

 WHAT YOU NEED

Peanuts in shell *(salted or unsalted)*
Googly eyes *(honestly, haven't you always
                    wanted an excuse to buy some?)*
Colored felt
Cardboard
Marker *(with sharp tip)*
Cardboard jewelry box
Glue gun

INSTRUCTIONS

The Stage

1. Purchase jewelry solely to obtain cardboard box for this craft. *(You may keep the jewelry.)*
2. Cut out a square from the lid and, using the leftover square, cut out an oval. On this, write or paint the words "Peanut Gallery."

INSTRUCTIONS

The Stage (continued)

3. Cut out felt curtains for the opening and glue in place.
4. Draw an appropriate backdrop in the back of the box.
5. Set lid and box aside.

The Peanuts

6. Select a variety of peanuts and glue on googly eyes.*
7. Using marker, connect with your inner Michelangelo and draw the expressions you would expect from your Peanut Gallery after hearing your tales of woe. Suggestions include shock, horror, amusement, rage, and anguish.

The Risers

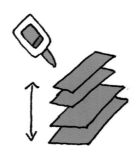

8. Cut 2 strips of cardboard to make the top riser. *It should be as wide as the jewelry box and less than half its depth.*
9. Cut 2 strips of cardboard for the bottom riser. *It should be as wide and as deep as the jewelry box.*
10. Glue risers together as shown.
11. Cut a piece of felt "carpet" and glue onto the steps.

Assembly

12. Glue half of your peanut friends onto the top riser and the other half onto the bottom riser.
13. Glue the peanuts and their risers into the cardboard box.
14. Glue the lid onto the box.
15. Glue the Peanut Gallery sign on the box.

Voilà! Your Peanut Gallery.

* BONUS CRAFT
Glue googly eyes onto other inanimate objects for more general levity.

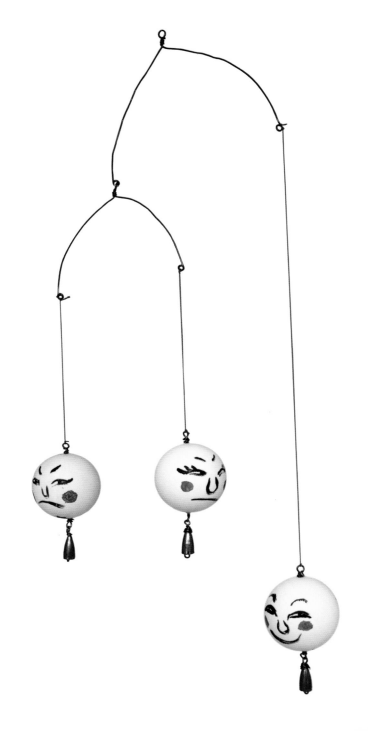

Ping-Pong Emotional Mobile

For when you don't know if you're coming or going

Express your inner emotional conflict with this nifty mobile.

WHAT YOU NEED

3 ping-pong balls
20-gauge wire *(found in most craft stores)*
Lead fishing weights
Enamel poster paint or permanent markers
Embroidery floss
Soothing scented candle
Large needle *(longer than the diameter of the ping-pong balls)*
Pliers

INSTRUCTIONS

1. Set the mood by lighting the scented candle and turning on
    your favorite radio station or popping in a relaxing CD.

2. With the pliers, hold the needle and heat the sharp tip over a flame. Quickly, before the needle cools, poke a hole through the top and bottom of each ping-pong ball.* You will need 3 ping-pong balls, but we suggest you go ahead and poke the six you likely purchased— just in case.

    > *** HEADS UP**
    >
    > You'll hear an alarming sizzling sound when you poke the ping pong ball with the hot needle. Do not panic. The needle isn't hot enough to turn the ball into a fiery weapon of mass destruction, and if you freak out and drop it, the ball will skitter all over your room, making it hard to retrieve.

3. Cut 3 pieces of wire, each 5 inches in length. Thread these through the ping-pong balls, creating a loop on both ends and attaching a fishing lead weight on one of the ends as shown below.

    Tip: Put the ping-pong ball against a light to thread the wire.

4. Using enamel paint or a marker, paint or draw faces onto each side of the ping-pong ball. Do this for all 3 balls. Let the face dry on one side of the ball before attempting another, or it will smear.

4. (continued)

Face suggestions:

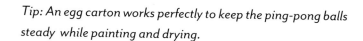

- Hysterical Laughing Face
- Depressed My Life Is Over Face
- I Have No Emotion Left in Me Face

Tip: An egg carton works perfectly to keep the ping-pong balls steady while painting and drying.

5. For the mobile, cut a 6-inch and 7-inch length of wire. Twist the wire in the shapes as shown at left, attaching the smaller arm onto the larger arm.

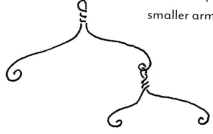

6. Attach embroidery floss to the wire at the top of each ball, then attach the balls to the arms.

Voilà! Your Ping-Pong Emotional Mobile.

Getting through the Holidays

When you don't feel like ho, ho, hoing

Even if you're a scheduling pro whose smartphone is always synced with her tablet, one thing is for sure: Your break up will come at the worst possible time. And there's nothing you can do about it.

Without fail, break ups occur right before Christmas, New Year's Eve, or, worst of all, on or near Valentine's Day. To add to your distress, everywhere you look—crammed in stores, restaurants, and sidewalks—you'll see happy couples who have chosen to crawl out of the woodwork at that exact moment, so you can feel your despair even more keenly.

A little holiday crafting, however, can help. With just a swipe of a handy eyeliner or eyebrow liner from your cosmetic bag you can create a sad, angry, or ambivalent Santa ornament (or other holiday icon, pagan or otherwise). If it is indeed the dreaded Valentine's Day, note the photo at left—with a little strategically placed construction paper, you can still enjoy the holiday, your way.

"Blue
Oh, so lonesome for you.
Why can't you be blue over me?"
— LeAnn Rimes
Lyrics by Bill Mack

Activities for the Despairing

Whether he cheated on you, or decided he just didn't love you "that way," or found his true love in the gutter by a dumpster—or even if you decided to leave him—that kicked-in-the-gut feeling is terrible. Even though we all know you're better off without the lying, cheating, no good, lily-livered, yellow-bellied, egg-sucking dog, we also know that it just plain feels bad.

Some well-meaning friends, or perhaps your mother, will say that the best course is to put on a brave face and tough it out. We believe in the opposite: Just wallow in feeling bad until you feel better.

Doing some of the activities in this section will help with the wallowing. So get the tissues out along with your crafting supplies and start crying and creating.

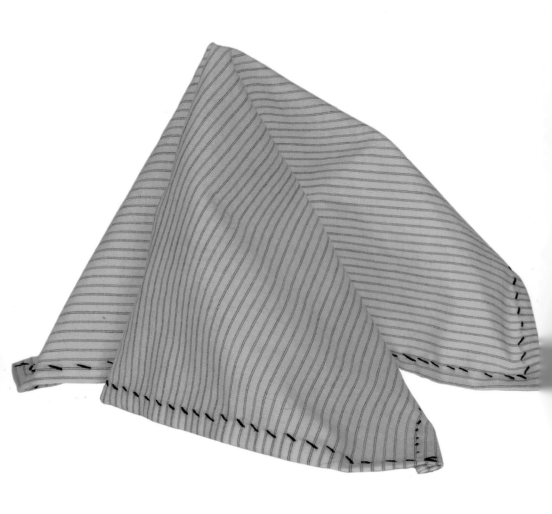

Weepy Wipes

"Alone and crying, crying, crying, crying"
Roy Orbison & Joe Melson

Have you ever noticed that when you cry—really cry—your tears actually burn your face? That's why you need exceptionally soft hankies to wipe them away, and upcycling your ex's best shirts is sure to do the trick.

WHAT YOU NEED

Your ex's favorite dress shirts that were left behind—*oops!*
Contrasting embroidery floss

INSTRUCTIONS

1. Cut a 6.5 x 6.5-inch square* out of the flat part of shirt.

2. Press with a hot iron, then press corners of square as shown.

3. Roll edges in 1/4 inch on each side and embroider with floss.

Voilà! Your Weepy Wipes.

* FUN TIP
You may make your hankies different sizes, depending on the volume of tears you're shedding.

Why Are You Still Single Rejoinders

"The first thing I do in the morning is brush my teeth
and sharpen my tongue"
Dorothy Parker

Whether it's from a well-intentioned friend, a hopelessly clueless family member, a member of the Singles Police, or a back-biting, malicious frenemy, know that *you will be* confronted about your single status—especially when your feelings are at their rawest. Instead of immediately bursting into tears, take the time now to prepare a few snappy comebacks. And then cry afterward, privately.

HELPFUL TIP
During this period of despair, make sure you always have allergy eye drops on hand (to get the redness out of your eyes) and touch-up makeup so you can reapply the spackle after you've cried it off.

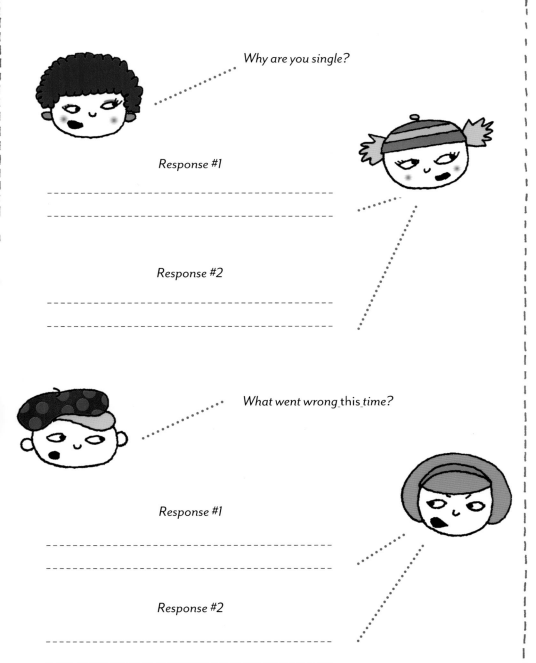

Why are you single?

Response #1

Response #2

What went wrong this time?

Response #1

Response #2

You're lucky—I wish I was single.

Response #1

Response #2

Are you gay?

Response #1

Response #2

And that's just the beginning. Here are a few more gems requiring advance preparation.

Maybe you're not trying hard enough.

Your Response

When are you getting married?

Your Response

There are plenty of fish in the sea.

Your Response

Beggars can't be choosers.

Your Response

Pity Party

"It's my party and I'll cry if I want to"
Sung by Leslie Gore

Don't you hate it when people tell you to "just get over it"—and you just aren't over it? We recommend you give yourself permission to feel and to celebrate—that's right, celebrate feeling sorry for yourself—for as long as you want.

WHAT YOU NEED

Old wrapping paper
Yarn

INSTRUCTIONS

1. Cut wrapping paper into squares. The squares can be different sizes.

2. Follow instructions on the following page to make origami balloons.

3. String balloons on yarn and decorate your office or living room or wherever you want to hold your pity party.

Voilà! You're ready to start your Pity Party.

INSTRUCTIONS

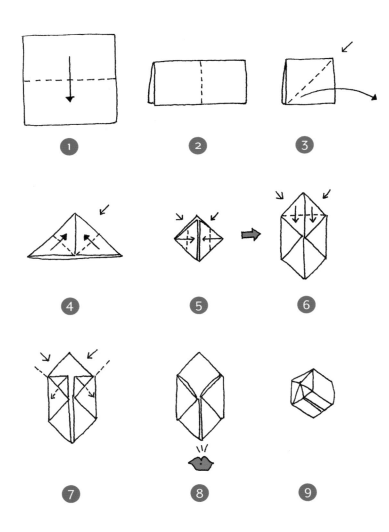

FUN TIP

Misery Loves Company

Pity parties do not need to be limited to just you. In fact, the more the merrier.

Invite your comrades in misery for an evening of supreme unhappiness. Have a sharing session in which each pal gets equal time to whine about the subject of his or her choosing, and follow up the whining with a supportive discussion. Next, write each of your sorrows on a slip of paper—and at the end of the night, go pyro and watch your issues turn into ash!

Refreshments should include ample offerings from the four universal survival food groups: salt, fat, sugar, and chocolate. Copious alcohol is also advised.

Make sure to share, gorge, and imbibe with impunity, because everyone knows that when you're miserable, calories don't count.

Don't Text Him Fill-in Blues

You know he's there. Or is he? Did he lie about what he was doing and, more importantly, with whom? Try to resist that urge to text him to find out with this easy-to-create blues lament.

WHAT YOU NEED

Blues CD of your choosing
Pen
The blues

INSTRUCTIONS

1. Put on your blues CD to get into the mood.

2. Fill in the blanks on the following page.

3. Start singing at the top of your lungs and feeling incredibly sorry for yourself.

   Voilà! You are singing the Don't Text Him Fill-in Blues.

It's _____ in the morning,
time

and I haven't heard from U yet.

It's _____ in the morning,
time

did U not get my text?

I am so _____.
emotion

Is it the coverage? WTH?

YKW, I saw _____ on FB.
incident, picture

I can't believe my eyes.

I saw _____ on FB.
incident, picture

and U know FB don't lie.

I am so _____ baby.
emotion

All your text-cuses, they just don't satisfy.

I might have no self-esteem.

No _____ too.
*some critical
personality trait*

Even fast food and TiVo

are like making me _____ blue.
adjective

But I'm not going to text you at _____
time

because now I am YY4U.

Lucky Cap Tea Cozy

Keep your tea warm while crying into it

WHAT YOU NEED

1 lucky baseball cap
Buttons (for eyes)
Felt
Needle & thread
Stitch remover
Your favorite tea

INSTRUCTIONS

1. Remove the bill of the cap with the stitch remover, then hem the inside band.

2. Cut a hole in the cap (for the tea spout) and hem.

3. Cut the bill into two ear-shape pieces and attach to the cap.

4. Add a cute face with buttons and get as creative as you want with felt. Put the kettle on and make yourself a cuppa.

Voilà! Your Lucky Cap Tea Cozy.

Cashmere Cup Pup Cuff

At least your drink will feel loved

WHAT YOU NEED

Sleeve from his favorite cashmere sweater
Buttons
Needle & thread

INSTRUCTIONS

1. Cut the cuffs off sweater. *(Bonus: Since the sleeves were likely too long for you anyway, you can still wear the sweater.)*

2. Cut two ears and muzzle out of one cuff and discard the rest of the cuff.

* BE CREATIVE
Make different animals and creatures and astound your friends.

3. Sew the ears, muzzle, button eyes, and button nose onto the remaining cuff.*

Voilà! Your Cashmere Cup Pup Cuff.

"Here's all you have to know about men and women: Women are crazy, men are stupid. And the main reason women are crazy is that men are stupid."
— George Carlin

Anger, Anger, Anger

You saw the battalion of red flags from the start—your friends never did like him, your family never approved, and deep down in your heart, you knew a break up was inevitable. Even so, there's nothing quite as satisfying as refusing to take any personal responsibility and blaming it all on your ex. So why not just embrace all that pent-up outrage and focus on the myriad ways you've been slighted by the bum?

That's where the crafts and activities in this section come in. They allow you to make creative, practical use of all that negative energy that otherwise would be directed toward things that might end up on your permanent record (or worse, on Twitter), preventing you from ever being gainfully employed again.

Of course, we hope that while you channel these intense emotions into our vengeful yet oh-so-harmless crafts, your anger begins to dissipate, and you find yourself moving to a calmer, more transcendental place ... NOT!

Cuban Cigar Cabin

A classic stogie abode

With this satisfying craft, you repurpose those cigars he doted on while neglecting your real-life needs.

WHAT YOU NEED

22 high-quality cigars *(approximately 6 inches long)**

Corrugated cardboard

Foam core

Heavy paper stock

Toothpick

Red & green construction paper

* HOT TIP
This craft works best with Cuban cigars.

INSTRUCTIONS

The Cabin

1. Carefully remove the bands around the cigars. You will need to use these later for the fence.

2. Cut a 4.25 x 4.25-inch square out of the foam core. This will be the "foundation" of your cabin.

3. Just like with logs in a real log cabin, you'll need to cut notches into each cigar. The best way to ensure that all the cigars have notches in the same place is to make a little frame out of foam core, as shown at right.

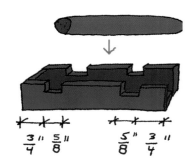

Exact measurements are not necessary, but the frame should hold the cigar tightly and have two notches about 5/8 inches wide (the diameter of the cigar) × 1/4 inch deep, 3/4 inches from each end of the frame as shown. Leave one end of the frame open.

4. Place the cigars into the frame one at a time and cut notches. You will need 11 notched cigars, plus more unnotched ones for the roof.

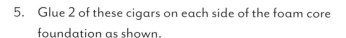

5. Glue 2 of these cigars on each side of the foam core foundation as shown.

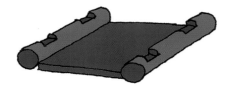

6. Assemble the cabin, 2 cigars per row, putting the final 3 logs on top, notches down. You may need to jiggle the cigars and use a little hot glue to stabilize your frame.

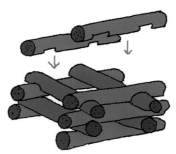

The Roof

7. Cut 2 triangles (gables) 6.5 inches wide and 3 inches tall out of the corrugated cardboard about the width of the cabin. Pencil in 5 notches along the roof line and 3 notches along the base (where it will rest on the frame of the house) and cut out.

8. Place gables on the frame and then add unnotched cigars along the roof. Again, a little hot glue will help stabilize the roof.

High Realism

9. Assemble a flag using the toothpick and construction paper, cut out a cardboard door, and glue both on the cabin. Glue the cigar bands onto heavy card stock and assemble them. As the pièce de résistance, add some grass to the fence.

Tip: Add a sliver of foam core behind the fence so it will stand up.

Voilà! Your Cuban Cigar Cabin.

Victorian Cameo Cutting Board

Just perfect for slicing and dicing

This simple cutting board makes for a most excellent kitchen work surface, especially when you're preparing that *last* meal —if you get our drift.

WHAT YOU NEED

Plain wooden cutting board
Small can of black enamel paint
Sealer

INSTRUCTIONS

1. Draw your ex's silhouette on the cutting board in pencil. Feel free to improvise (devil horns, warts, nose hair).

2. Use enamel paint to fill in the silhouette.

3. When the paint is dry, add a few coats of sealer. Make sure the board is thoroughly dry before using.

Voilà! Your Victorian Cameo Cutting Board is ready for chopping, mincing, and cutting to the core.

Baseball House of Cards

Stack and interlock together for hours of fun

You never understood the obsession with them. And now it's time to free them from their silly plastic sleeves.

WHAT YOU NEED

Baseball card collection
Permanent marker
Exacto knife

INSTRUCTIONS

1. With an exacto knife, cut 6 1/2-inch long x 1/8-inch wide slots on each card as shown.

   Tip: This works best if all the slots are equal distances apart, so measure your first card and use it as a template for the others.

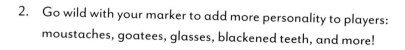

2. Go wild with your marker to add more personality to players: moustaches, goatees, glasses, blackened teeth, and more!

   Voilà! Your Baseball House of Cards.

Rewriting History Rejoinders

Frustrated that you were too overwhelmed to get in the last word? Did you think of the perfect comeback to showcase your barbed wit only after you stormed off? Release that negative energy and empower your inner child by writing down the witty, stinging retort you would have delivered if only you'd had the time to prepare.

THE SITUATION

_____

_____

_____

What your ex said

_____

_____

_____

What you wish you said

_____

_____

_____

THE SITUATION

What your ex said

What you wish you said

Famous Comebacks

Noel Coward: "You almost look like a man."
Edna Ferber: " So do you."

Young Man: " I can't bear fools."
Dorothy Parker: "Apparently your mother could."

THE SITUATION

What your ex said

What you wish you said

Famous Comeback

Nancy Astor: "Winston, if you were my husband, I'd poison your coffee."

Winston Churchill: "Nancy, if you were my wife, I'd drink it."

Word Scrambler

For some easygoing fun, pull out a pen and find the words
in the letters below.

```
Z  P  W  A  T  L  O  S  E  R  A  T
V  M  O  R  O  N  Z  E  I  C  N  R
A  G  R  E  E  D  Y  L  M  S  N  O
I  V  T  L  I  A  R  F  M  T  O  B
N  C  H  E  A  T  B  C  A  U  Y  Q
O  B  L  S  N  A  K  E  T  P  I  U
C  R  E  E  P  E  A  N  U  I  N  R
L  E  S  L  O  U  D  T  T  D  G  I
U  I  S  F  O  T  D  E  R  W  T  D
E  H  Y  I  G  N  O  R  A  N  T  I
S  M  E  S  S  Y  P  E  H  X  J  O
M  X  C  H  N  M  E  D  I  C  K  T
```

Did we miss any words you'd like to add?

Cut & Paste Revenge

Revenge is sweet, but not if you end up in jail. With some scissors and a glue stick, you can do someharmless wishful thinking.

WHAT YOU NEED

Photos of your ex
Scissors
Glue stick

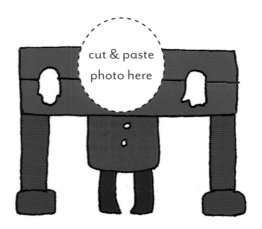

cut & paste
photo here

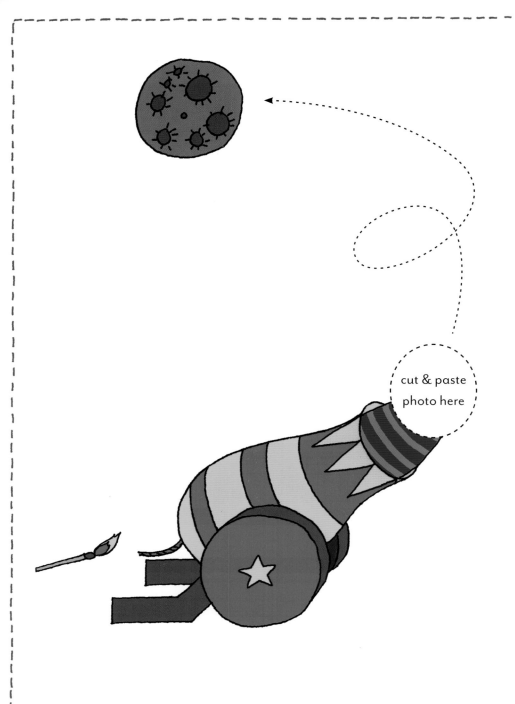

cut & paste
photo here

cut & paste
photo here

Drive-by Bingo

More fun than going to Zumba

WHAT YOU NEED

Cardboard
Magic marker
Sticker paper
Exacto knife

INSTRUCTIONS

1. Cut out a 6 x 8.5-inch piece of cardboard. You may cut more pieces if you'd like to play with multiple cards. Write the word "BINGO" in magic marker on top of each card.

    Tip: If you use fewer cards, you can focus more on the game.

2. Photocopy the icons on the following pages onto sticker paper, cut them out, and randomly place on the cardboard sheets.

3. Drive by your ex's house, and look for the items on the board.

    Tip: You may wish to predetermine your prizes. We suggest jewelry or, if you're on a budget, chocolate.

    Voilà! Your Drive-by Bingo.

BINGO ICONS

Baseball Bat

Big Dog

Ex Sighting

Ex Super-Sighting

Dead Fish

Dead Fish
in Mailbox

Rotten Egg

Music

Motorcycle

Match

Fire

Pylon

Hammer

Light

Little Dog

Spray Paint

His Car

His Car with
Shaving Cream

Random
Flat Tire

His Car with Shaving
Cream & Flat Tire

Trash Can

Trash on Lawn

Tree

Unknown Car

DRAW YOUR OWN BINGO ICONS

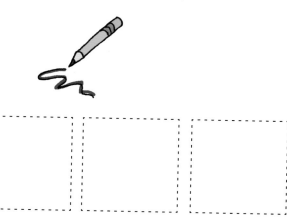

Voodoo Sock

Forget about the voodoo doll—that is so yesterday. A voodoo sock will give your ex a world of hex hurt without the need for any pins.

WHAT YOU NEED

Sock *(preferably from your ex's favorite pair)*
Iron-on transfer *(that you can print from your printer)*
Photo of ex, rubber ball, red yarn

INSTRUCTIONS

1. Print out your ex's photo on the iron-on transfer. Cut out photo and follow instructions to iron it onto the foot end of the sock.

2. Place rubber ball in sock and tie it closed with yarn.

3. Find a wall. With your back against the wall, use your right hand to swing the sock back and forth across your body, hitting the ball as hard as you can against the wall. Switch to your left hand and repeat.*

Voilà! Your Voodoo Sock.

* TONING TIP
Do 3 reps on each side for an incredible underarm exercise.

Favorite-sweater Punching Bag

"A boxing match is like a cowboy movie. There's got to be good guys and there's got to be bad guys. And that's what people pay for—to see the bad guys get beat"

Charles Liston

WHAT YOU NEED

Your ex's favorite sweater(s)
Grommet, needle & thread
Stuffing, sawdust, or shredded fabric
Speed punching-bag swivel

INSTRUCTIONS

1. Cut 4 pieces of sweater in pear shapes as shown.

2. Sew the 4 pieces together, inside out, leaving a small opening.

3. Turn the punching bag right side out, fill it, and sew opening closed.

4. Apply the grommet and embellish with sweater scraps.

5. Attach to the punching-bag swivel.

Voilà! Your Favorite-sweater Punching Bag.

Badly Woven Photo Memory

So surprisingly easy to create a modern masterpiece

WHAT YOU NEED

2 photos of ex
Exacto knife
Tape *(optional)*

INSTRUCTIONS

1. Cut one photo in equal-width vertical strips and the other in equal-width horizontal strips.

2. Weave the strips together.*

   Tip: Taping the edge of one photo helps make the weaving easier.

   * BONUS CRAFT
   Arrange the photo scraps into a pyre and ignite them safely in your kitchen sink.

3. Place in frame and give your creation a great name.

   Voilà! Your Badly Woven Photo Memory.

Get-a-Golf-Grip Coasters

Such a delightful variety of colors and patterns!

WHAT YOU NEED

Golf grips
Clear epoxy
Exacto knife

INSTRUCTIONS

1. Remove golf grips from clubs.* Carefully place clubs back into bag.

2. Using an exacto knife, cut the grips into 1/2-inch rounds.

3. Arrange rounds into a pleasing coaster pattern.

4. Epoxy the rounds together and allow the epoxy to set.

* BONUS CRAFT
Do not remove the grip from the putter. Instead, give it a very, very slight, *unnoticeable to the naked eye*, bend.

Voilà! Your Get-a-Golf-Grip Coasters.

"Muddy waters, let stand, become clear."

—Lao-Tsu

Rejoining the Living

The journey from the initial shock to accepting the finality of a break up takes time. So give yourself permission to take that time, and be prepared for it to mean taking two steps forward and one step back—or one step forward and two steps back.

But you will heal. You'll know you're improving when you not only feel better about yourself but actually feel more *like* yourself. You won't wince when you see happy couples walking down the street or hear "your" song on the radio. Life will seem positive again, and you'll look forward to what the future may hold.

On that day, when you wake up to a sunny sky studded with fluffy clouds, you will also realize that it really was all for the best—and, more importantly, all the good things everyone has been telling you about yourself while you've been suffering...

All true.

A Tool's God's Eye

A twist on the yarn-woven spiritual art form originating with the Huichol Indians of Jalisco, Mexico

WHAT YOU NEED

His (leftover) tools
Yarn
20-gauge wire
2 decorative bells

INSTRUCTIONS

1. You may remember doing this with popsicle sticks, but because tools are heavier, you must stabilize the cross by wiring the tools together as shown. Tie the wires tightly.

2. Flip the tools over, so the tied wire end is on the back, and then tightly wrap the tools with yarn as shown.

3. When you're finished, tie on the bells.

    Tip: We used wrenches for our craft, but you can substitute other tools.

    Voilà! A Tool's God's Eye.

Tie Sachets

***There's nothing quite like working
with exquisite European silks***

WHAT YOU NEED

Silk ties
Stitch remover
Needle & thread
Potpourri

INSTRUCTIONS

1. Remove all the backing from each tie with the stitch remover and discard.

2. Iron the silk tie fabric flat and cut into 4-inch squares. You'll need 2 squares per sachet.

3. By hand or with a sewing machine, sew the squares together, with the back side of the fabric facing out. Leave a small hole so you can turn the squares right side out.

4. Turn the squares right side out, fill with your favorite potpourri, and hem in the opening.

Voilà! Your Tie Sachets.

These Boots Are Made for Planting

So easy, your ex could make it

WHAT YOU NEED

Pair of shoes
Plastic liner
2 plants

INSTRUCTIONS

1. Line the shoes with plastic liner (otherwise they will soon smell worse than they already do, plus they'll fall apart).

2. Insert 1 plant in each shoe. Don't forget to water regularly.

DECORATING TIP
Adorable next to your welcome mat, and such a conversation piece, too!

Voilà! Your These Boots Are Made for Planting.

Take-the-Power Superhero Jock Mask

"Sometimes in life you don't always feel like a winner, but that doesn't mean you're not a winner"
Lady Gaga

WHAT YOU NEED

Jock strap *(the "special" one he's won everything in)*
Exacto knife
Hot-melt glue or clear epoxy
Spray paint
Self-stick "power" gems
Ribbon

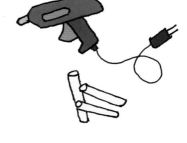

INSTRUCTIONS

1. Remove the plastic cup from the jock strap and discard the strap part.

2. Do whatever you need to do to sterilize the cup, from bleaching it overnight to running it through the dishwasher a million times.

3. Cut the cup portion exactly in half as shown.

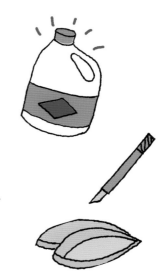

Tip: Take several passes with your cutting instead of trying to cut through the plastic the first time.

4. Position the pieces into a pleasing mask shape.
    Then pencil in the eyes and cut out with an exacto knife,
    making sure you clean up rough edges.

5. Cut notches for the ribbon.

6. Assemble the pieces together and hot glue or epoxy together.

7. Spray paint the mask and allow it to dry
    completely overnight.

8. Attach the ribbons and have fun decorating
    your mask with your power self-stick gems.

Voilà! Your Take-the-Power Superhero Jock Mask.

FUN TIP

Your superhero costume doesn't need to stop with this mask. While in private (or not), consider adding black leggings, stilettos, a cape, and, of course, bright red nail polish. Or whatever makes you feel confident, capable, and empowered.

You can create a public superhero costume as well. Build it around a special outfit, a great pair of shoes, or your favorite jeans. In time, you'll find that you don't need your outfit anymore—you'll finally understand, like the real superheroes do, that the power isn't found in your costume, but within yourself.

"If you want your life to be more rewarding, you have to change the way you think."
— Oprah Winfrey

Things to Do & Try

It can be quite a shock to find yourself doing the things you used to do together all by yourself. But though it may be scary at first, you'll soon learn to love it—now you get to do whatever *you* want, whenever you want. A few ideas:

- Take a trip to a nearby city or a foreign country
- Learn an exotic language
- Take up surfing and consider a rad new life as a beach bum
- Face your fears by jumping from a plane
- Learn to skateboard to the corner store
- Amaze your friends and family at weddings and social gatherings by learning some fancy footwork at a ballroom dancing class
- Remember that restaurant you've wanted to try, but he wasn't interested? Get gussied up and treat yourself—and don't be stingy on dessert
- Get a membership at a gym; if you already have one, start pumping iron or try a new class
- Get in touch with nature by hiking in your nearest park or forest
- Take a cooking class and become an expert in making something exotic, like bonbons
- Learn to paint, and fill your home with your own stunning artwork

Your Happy-to-Be-Alone To Do List

1. _____
   _____

2. _____
   _____

3. _____
   _____

4. _____
   _____

5. _____
   _____

6. _____
   _____

7. _____
   _____

8. _____
   _____

9. _____
   _____

10. _____
    _____

Words of Wisdom

"Sometimes you can't see yourself clearly until you see yourself through the eyes of others"
Ellen DeGeneres

WHAT YOU NEED

Your biggest fans

INSTRUCTIONS

1. Ask your closest friends and family members to write down what they love most about you on the pages that follow. Attach your favorite snapshots of them and/or both of you above their comments.

2. If you run out of room, which of course you will, photocopy the following pages and have them record their comments.

Voilà! Your Words of Wisdom.

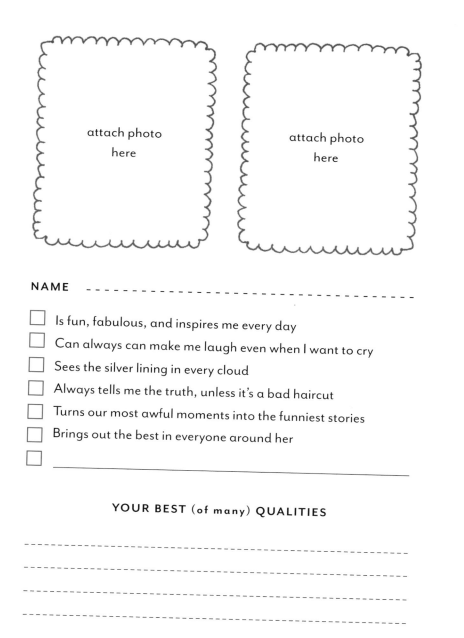

attach photo
here

attach photo
here

NAME -

☐ Is fun, fabulous, and inspires me every day

☐ Can always can make me laugh even when I want to cry

☐ Sees the silver lining in every cloud

☐ Always tells me the truth, unless it's a bad haircut

☐ Turns our most awful moments into the funniest stories

☐ Brings out the best in everyone around her

☐ _____

YOUR BEST (of many) QUALITIES

- -

- -

- -

- -

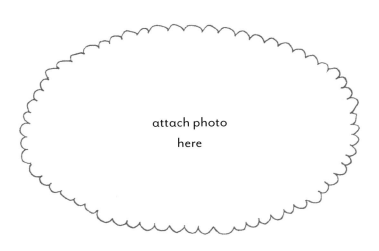

attach photo
here

NAME -

☐ Lent me her favorite _____without a thought

☐ Accepts me for who I am

☐ Eats ice cream with me for hours without mentioning calories

☐ Gives the best advice, from financial tips to what to wear on
Saturday night

☐ Brings beauty and grace to everything she does

☐ _____

SOMETHING FUNNY

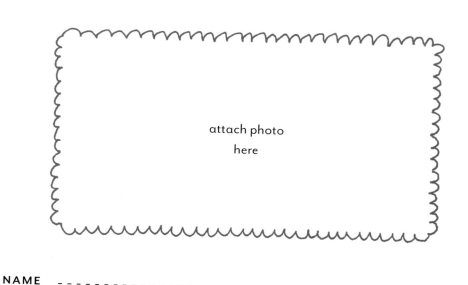

attach photo
here

NAME -

- [ ] Still giggles even though she is a grown, capable, and successful woman
- [ ] Is caring and kind but still hates my enemies more than I do
- [ ] Befriended me when I was the shy, new kid on the playground
- [ ] Takes chances and makes every day an adventure
- [ ] Always finds the time to help her friends
- [ ] Makes everyone around her feel special
- [ ] _____

A MEMORABLE MOMENT

- -

- -

- -

- -

Bits & Pieces but Still Dancing Boa

Shake it until you make it

WHAT YOU NEED

Crafting scraps from his shirts and sweaters
Yarn
Jingle bells
Dance music

INSTRUCTIONS

1. Cut some of your scraps into a couple of dozen long pieces, about 1.5 x 6 inches. (*Tip: Making scraps different lengths will make your boa more interesting.*) Cut more scraps into circles, squares, or whatever shapes strikes your fancy, about 3 inches in diameter, and cut a small hole in the center of each of these smaller scraps.

2. Cut a length of yarn appropriate for a boa—long enough so you can toss it saucily over your shoulder.

3. Tie a bell on one end. Tie the longer scraps onto the yarn and intersperse stringing on the smaller ones, in whatever pattern pleases you. Place small bells randomly. Put a bell on the end. Wrap around self and turn on the music. Loud. Shake it, baby!

Voilà! Your Bits & Pieces but Still Dancing Boa.

Remote Control Ramen Pirate Ship

Unless he's Johnny Depp, toss that memory overboard, matey

WHAT YOU NEED

2 remote controls *(oops, they accidentally fell out of his moving boxes!)*
Hot glue gun + exacto knife
2 packages ramen noodles *(from his junk-food stash)*
Wooden chopsticks
Black construction paper + opaque white marker

INSTRUCTIONS

1. Remove the battery cover from one of the remotes.
2. With a hacksaw, cut one of the remotes in half and hot-glue the two pieces and the battery cover onto the remaining remote.
3. Using an exacto knife, dig out two center rubber buttons from the base remote for the chopstick masts and hot-glue them into place.
4. Use both ramen packages and one flavor packet for the sails by cutting holes on the top and bottom and fitting them over the chopstick masts.
5. Cut a flag out of black construction paper and, using your white marker, draw a skull and bones. Glue onto chopstick.

Ahoy! Your Remote Control Ramen Pirate Ship.

The Running-into Speech

"Be Prepared"
Boy Scout Motto

No matter how much you think you're over him, nothing will shatter your hard-won peace of mind more than running into your ex when you least expect it. He's certain to be with his new supermodel-looking doctor/lawyer/astronaut girlfriend, and inevitably they will have just returned from a tropical vacation and will be sporting matching tans, smiles, and possibly engagement rings. You, of course, will be having an exceptionally horrific day, will be dressed in sweats, and will still be single.

Your choices? Sure, you could run away, duck into a nearby alley, or turn nasty and spiteful. But that won't help. Instead, take the high road and practice your fiction-writing skills. Just make sure you've written and rehearsed your diva-worthy reponse to, "How are you?"

- -
- -
- -
- -
- -
- -
- -
- -
- -

Preflight Dating Checklist

You know you're ready to start dating again when:

☐ You've deleted the compare-my-ex app from your smartphone.

☐ Your emotional baggage is now TSA-approved carry-on size.

☐ You realize that not every comment is directed at you personally, including the ones at the checkout at your local market.

☐ You stop equating being perfect with being happy.

☐ You know that you don't need someone else to be the fabulous person you are.

☐ --

☐ --

☐ --

Happily Ever After
Cut & Paste

When you're ready—and only when you're ready—it will be time to acknowledge that you are your own hero. No longer will you be waiting for that knight in shining armor, because that knight is already within you.

WHAT YOU NEED

Photo of self
Scissors
Glue

INSTRUCTIONS

1.   Cut out your face and paste in the picture on the right.

Voilà! You are your own hero.

cut & paste photo here

Super Chocolate Brownies

"A little too much chocolate is just about right"

5 ounces unsweetened (99%) chocolate

5 ounces 72% dark chocolate

1/2 pound (2 sticks) butter

5 eggs

1 teaspoon vanilla extract

1 1/4 cups granulated sugar

3/4 cup brown sugar

1 1/2 cups all-purpose flour

1 1/2 teaspoons baking powder

3/4 teaspoon salt

Powdered sugar for dusting (optional)

1. Preheat oven to 325 degrees.

2. In the bowl of a double boiler, melt the chocolate and butter. Stir until smooth. Let cool for 5 minutes.

3. In the bowl of a large mixer fitted with a paddle attachment, mix the eggs and vanilla. Gradually add the sugars and mix just until loosely combined.

4. Drizzle in the chocolate mixture and mix until combined.

5. Combine flour, baking soda, and salt in a separate bowl and add to mixer. Blend until combined.

6. Coat an 8 x 8-inch pan with vegetable spray.

7. Pour batter into pan. Bake for 20 minutes, rotate pan, and bake for another 15-20 minutes or until a toothpick inserted in the middle comes out clean.

8. Remove and allow brownies to cool before cutting.

9. Dust with powdered sugar.

Enjoy!

Adapted from Little Flower: Recipes from the Cafe

BROWNIE HEAVEN

Experiment! Add a teaspoon of cayenne to spice them up or a dash of cinnamon or cardamom to make them more exotic. A few tablespoons of beer, bourbon, or Triple Sec will give them a more adult spin. And, of course, adding chocolate chips, nuts, caramels, or M&M's is a no-brainer.

Consider turning your brownie into a sundae with ice cream, whipped cream, chocolate sauce, nuts, sprinkles, and a cherry on top.

If you overcook the brownies, don't worry. Just make the equivalent of brownie lemonade. Create sandwiches by placing a scoop of ice cream between two brownies, and make it gourmet by adding a layer of fruit jam.

The possibilities are endless. Just like with your new life!

CERTIFICATE OF COMPLETION

This certifies that

_____
Name

has NOT texted, internet-stalked, tweeted, or abused any other form of social media as regards her ex, nor has she spied on, driven by, or obsessively talked about her ex with friends, family, or total strangers, for:

(check all that apply)

☐ a New York minute   ☐ a day

☐ an hour   ☐ a week

☐ almost 2 hours   ☐ a month

at _____ on this _____ day of _____
    location   *day*   *month*

in the year _____
          year

CERTIFICATE OF COMPLETION

This certifies that

_____
Name

has SURVIVED her (1st, 2nd, 3rd, 4th, 5th, 6th, 7th)
please circle one or write in number here _____

break up and has not given up or surrendered, is still moving,
and now understands from the top of her head to the tip of her toes that what doesn't kill you
makes you stronger—especially if chocolate is involved.

at _____ on this _____ day of _____
    location   *day*   *month*

in the year _____
       year

ABOUT THE AUTHOR

Lynn Chang may be happily married now, but she knows her way around a broken heart—and the value of a good revenge craft. She has written and/or illustrated many books, including *Look at Me! Animals* (Chronicle), *Yoga for Cats* (Chronicle), and *Disguises for Your Dog* (St. Martin's). She also likes to play in clay, with paint, or in the garden, and she also plays the piano. Her favorite color is blue, and she lives in Southern California with her menagerie of finches, doves, goldfishes, William the Cat, and her husband, Fox.